THIS BOOK
BELONGS TO

KINGFISHER

Saints
and
Angels

Claire Llewellyn

KINGFISHER
BOSTON

KINGFISHER

a Houghton Mifflin Company imprint
222 Berkeley Street
Boston, Massachusetts 02116
www.houghtonmifflinbooks.com

First published in 2003
Reprinted in a revised format in 2006
2 4 6 8 10 9 7 5 3 1
1TR/1105/THOM/THOM/150SINMA/CTP

LIBRARY OF CONGRESS CATALOGING-IN-PUBLICATION DATA
Llewellyn, Claire.
Saints and Angels / by Claire Llewellyn.—1st ed.
p. cm.
Includes index.
Summary: A collection of brief profiles and pictures of nearly thirty saints, descriptions
of different kinds of angels, profiles of three specific angels, and a calendar of feast days.
What is a saint?—Holy family—Followers of Christ—Gospel writers—
Martyrs—Great thinkers and evangelists—Peace and healing—Angels—Archangels.
1. Christian saints—Biography—Juvenile literature. 2. Angels—Juvenile literature. [1.
Saints 2. Angels.] I. Title.

BX4658.L54 2003
270.092'2—dc21
[B]   2002034030

ISBN 0-7534-5906-X
ISBN 978-07534-5906-5

Consultant: Annette Reynolds at AD Publishing Services
Editor: Carron Brown
Coordinating editor: Stephanie Pliakas
Senior designer: Jane Tassie
Picture researcher: Rachael Swann
DTP coordinator: Sarah Pfitzner
DTP operator: Primrose Burton
Artwork archivists: Wendy Allison, Steve Robinson
Production controller: Debbie Otter
Indexer: Chris Bernstein

Printed in China

Acknowledgments
The publishers would like to thank the following for supplying photographs for this book:
b = bottom, *c* = center, *l* = left, *t* = top, *m* = middle, *r* = right
cover and presentation page: The National Gallery, London; pages: 1 The Bridgeman Art Library, London; 3 *tr* AKG London/S. Domingie;
4 *tl* AKG London/Cameraphoto; 4 *br* Scala; 5 *t* The National Gallery, London; 6 The National Gallery, London; 7 *tr* Scala; 8 *bl* AKG London;
9 *tl* Scala; 10 *tl* AKG London/Cameraphoto; 11 AKG London/Erich Lessing; 12 The National Gallery, London; 13 *tr* Scala; 15 The Art Archive/Fine
Art Museum, Bilbao/Dagli Orti (A); 16 Scala; 17 *br* The Art Archive/Dagli Orti; 18 *bl* The National Gallery, London; 19 *br*
The National Gallery, London; 20 *bl* The Art Archive/Biblioteca Nazionale Marciana, Venice/Dagli Orti (A); 21 *tl* AKG London/Cameraphoto;
22 *cr* AKG London/S. Domingie; 23 *br* Scala; 24 The Bridgeman Art Library/Galleria Borghese, Rome, Italy; 26 *bl* The National Gallery, London; 27
The Art Archive/Accademia Carrara, Bergamo, Italy/Dagli Orti; 28 *bl* The National Gallery, London; 29 *r* The National Gallery, London; 30 *bl* AKG
London; 31 *tr* AKG Berlin/S.Domingie; 32 Bridgeman Giraudon/Lauros; 33 *tr* The Art Archive/MusZe Thomas DobZe, Nantes/Dagli Orti; 34 *cl* AKG
London/Cameraphoto; 35 Scala; 36 AKG London/Cameraphoto; 37 *tr* The Bridgeman Art Library, London/Huntington Library and Art Gallery, San
Marino, CA, USA; 38 *bl* Scala; 39 *tl* The Bridgeman Art Library, London/Fitzwilliam Museum, University of Cambridge, U.K.; 40 *bl* AKG
London/Erich Lessing; 41 The Art Archive; 43 *bl* The Bridgeman Art Library, London; 43 *tr* AKG London/Cameraphoto; 44 *bl* The Bridgeman Art
Library, London/Galleria Nazionale dell'Umbria, Perugia, Italy; 45 *br* The Bridgeman Art Library, London/Archives Charmet; 48 *bl* Scala; 49 *tr* AKG
London/Erich Lessing; 50 *tl* The Bridgeman Art Library/Cameraphoto Arte Venezia: 51 *bl* AKG London/Orsi Battaglini; 52 The National Gallery,
London; 53 *tr* AKG London/Erich Lessing; 54 *tl* The National Gallery, London; 54 *bm* The National Gallery, London; 55 The National Gallery,
London; 56 The National Gallery, London; 57 *tr* AKG London; 58 *tl* AKG London/Gilles Mermet; 59 AKG London/Erich Lessing; 60 *tl* The
Bridgeman Art Library, London/Huntington Library and Art Gallery, San Marino, CA; 60 *tr* AKG London; 60 *bl* The Art Archive; 61 *tr* AKG
London/Erich Lessing; 61 *cl* AKG London/Cameraphoto; 61 *br* Scala.

The publishers would like to thank the following for supplying illustrations for this book:
Pages: 25 *tr* Janos, Middletons; 43 *tr* Roger Kent. Borders by Vanessa Card.

CONTENTS

WHAT IS A SAINT?

The name "saint" is given to a Christian person who has died and is worthy of great honor and respect. The name comes from the Latin word *sanctus*, meaning holy.

The first people to be made saints were Christ's family, his apostles, and the early Christian martyrs in the first century. These people were very well-known and became saints by word of mouth. The saints were given a feast day— a day of celebration that fell on the anniversary of their death rather than their birth. After all death was the moment when the saints were taken into heaven.

With the passing centuries, however, it was less easy to decide who was and was not worthy of being a saint. Eventually, in 1170, the pope decided that he should approve all new saints in a process called canonization. This is still how people become saints today.

detail from St. Ambrose with donors and St. Louis, St. Peter, St. Paul, and St. Sebastian
Bartolomeo Vivarini (1432–1499) Galleria dell'Accademia, Venice, Italy

Feast day
November 1— known as All Saints' Day

detail from The crucifixion with the Virgin and saints
Fra Angelico (c. 1387–1455) Museo di San Marco, Florence, Italy

4

There are many thousands of saints from all walks of life—peasants, princesses, teachers, soldiers, writers, doctors. Some saints traveled and did good works; others started religious houses and lived lives of simplicity and prayer. Most of them had a special gift—of loving God, of caring for the needy, of healing or teaching, of patience and wisdom. While some saints' lives are little more than legend, others are all too real. Many of the early saints faced persecution, torture, and a brutal death.

For many Christians the saints play an important role. They were once human, just like us, with human weaknesses and fears. Now that they are in heaven, close to God, they may act as valuable go-betweens, watching over us, protecting us, caring and praying for us. The saints in this book led extraordinary lives. Most of them faced enormous problems and met death with courage and faith. As some of the world's most inspiring role models they can show us how to be better people.

THE VIRGIN MARY
WITH THE
APOSTLES AND
OTHER SAINTS
*Fra Angelico
(c. 1387–1455)
The National
Gallery, London,
England*

5

VIRGIN MARY

Mary is the most important of all the saints—a person so good and holy that she was chosen to be the mother of God's own son. Mary loved Jesus and, in spite of her trust in God, suffered greatly as she watched him die.

Mary lived in Nazareth, Galilee. She was a gentle young woman who was engaged to a carpenter named Joseph. One day the archangel Gabriel visited her and told her that she would have a baby who would be the Son of God. Mary was amazed but obediently replied, "I am God's servant, and I will do as he asks."

Months later, when the baby was due, Mary and Joseph traveled to Bethlehem to register for their taxes. The town was so busy that they had to stay in a stable, and this was where Jesus was born. Mary was overjoyed with her baby boy, and weeks later she took him to a temple and dedicated him to God.

Mary loved Jesus with all her heart. As he grew up she saw how special he was. She was with him when he performed his first miracle. They were both at a wedding in Cana in modern-day Israel when the wine ran out. Mary told Jesus about the problem, and he changed jars of water into wine!

Mary knew that Jesus was doing God's work on Earth. Still, she must have been very frightened when he was arrested and sentenced to death. She suffered with him as he died on the cross.

Mary knew about Jesus' ascension into heaven. Many Christians believe that she, too, was taken into heaven.

detail from
THE VIRGIN
AT PRAYER
*Sassoferrato
(1609–1685)
The National
Gallery, London,
England*

FEAST DAY

*August 15—
the day Mary is
believed to have
ascended into
heaven*

PATRON SAINT

*The entire
human race*

THE MADONNA OF HUMILITY
*Lippo di Dalmasio (c. 1352–1410/1421)
The National Gallery, London, England*

St. Joseph

Joseph is often shown with a flowering stick, a carpentry tool, or a lily.

FEAST DAY
March 19

PATRON SAINT

Carpenters
The church
Fathers of families
Social justice
Working men

Joseph was the husband of Mary, who is the mother of Jesus, and the protector of the Holy Family. Although he wasn't Jesus' birth father, he loved and taught the young boy as if he were his own son.

Joseph, a carpenter from Nazareth in Galilee, was engaged to Mary. He was a simple, honest, respectable man. He must have been surprised when Mary told him she was expecting a baby and amazed when an angel explained to him that the baby was the Son of God!

Joseph felt responsible for the Holy Family and always did his best to protect them. He found the stable where Jesus was born. He hurried the family to safety in Egypt after an angel warned him that King Herod was planning to murder all baby boys. Like any parent, Joseph did what he could to raise Jesus properly.

It is thought that Joseph must have died while Jesus was still young. We know nothing about Joseph in Jesus' adult life, and he was not there when Jesus was crucified.

THE HOLY FAMILY WITH THE LAMB
Raphael, originally Raffaello Sanzio (1483–1520)
Museo del Prado, Madrid, Spain

ST. ANNE

The legend of St. Anne tells how, after years of being childless, a holy woman had a daughter named Mary and became grandmother to the baby Jesus.

FEAST DAY
*July 26—
shared with
her husband,
St. Joachim*

PATRON SAINT
*Canada
Childless people
Grandmothers
Pregnant women*

There are no historical facts known about Anne, the woman who is said to be the mother of Mary. But, in the early centuries of Christianity, a story developed about her. She was said to be married to a man named Joachim, who lived in Nazareth in Galilee. After 20 years of marriage the couple had no children, which made them very unhappy. Then Joachim decided to go into the desert for 40 days and 40 nights to pray for a child. While he was away Anne was visited by an angel, who told her that God had heard their prayers and that they would have a child. Anne was so grateful when her daughter, Mary, was born that she dedicated her to God.

Anne's legend tells us that she was a loving mother who raised Mary to put her trust and faith in God. When Mary herself gave birth to a child, Anne was devoted to her grandson, Jesus.

St. John *the* Baptist

JOHN THE BAPTIST
Paolo Veronese,
real name
Paolo Caliari
(1528–1588)
Galleria Estense,
Modena, Italy

FEAST DAY

June 24

PATRON SAINT

Baptism
Farriers
Freeways

John the Baptist was a prophet who prepared people for the coming of a great leader called the Messiah. As soon as John saw Jesus he knew that he was God's chosen one—the Messiah.

John was the son of Zechariah and Elizabeth, Mary's cousin. One day, while Zechariah was in the temple, he was visited by the archangel Gabriel, who told him that his wife would have a son who would become a great prophet—a messenger of God.

John grew into a remarkable man. To prepare for life as a prophet he lived in the desert for many years, wearing a shirt made of coarse hair and eating nothing but locusts and honey. John became a powerful preacher, and huge crowds gathered to hear him speak. He told them to prepare for the arrival of the Messiah, a leader promised by God. He urged them to confess their sins and be baptized in the Jordan River. One day Jesus came to be baptized. John recognized him instantly—he was the Messiah!

John was fearless and outspoken, even of the rich and powerful. When King Herod Antipas married his brother's wife, Herodias, John protested and was sent to prison. Herodias hated John and wanted him dead. Her chance came when her daughter, Salome, danced for Herod and was offered a gift in return. Salome, acting on her mother's behalf, asked for John's head. Instantly, the order went out, and the prophet was beheaded.

THE BAPTISM OF CHRIST
Joachim Patinier (c. 1475/1480–1524)
Kunsthistorisches Museum, Vienna, Austria

St. Mary Magdalene

Mary Magdalene was a devoted friend of Jesus and was with him when he died. Days later her sorrow turned to joy as she became the first person to see him rise from the dead.

MOLI ME TANGERE
*Beato Angelico
(1387–1455)
Museo di San Marco,
Florence, Italy*

Mary Magdalene lived in a small town by the Sea of Galilee. She suffered from a horrible illness caused by seven devils. One day she was cured by Jesus when he visited her town. Immediately, she was baptized a Christian, and she became his devoted follower. She was with Jesus at his crucifixion and stayed with him and his mother until the moment he died.

    Two days later Mary and some other women went to the tomb to anoint Jesus' body with perfumes and spices. When they got there, they found the tomb empty, with the huge stone that was blocking the entrance rolled away. Mary, heartbroken by the loss, sat weeping by the tomb.

    Soon a man came up to comfort her. She thought he was just the gardener, but when he gently spoke her name, she realized it was Jesus! He told her to go and tell his disciples that he had risen from the dead. With her heart full of joy, Mary ran to Jesus' friends to tell them the good news.

    Nothing more is known about Mary. One legend says she sailed west to present-day France, where she became a preacher; another says she traveled east with St. John and the Virgin Mary to the ancient Greek city of Ephesus, where she eventually died.

FEAST DAY
July 22

PATRON SAINT
*Repentant
sinners*

THE MAGDALEN
*around 1530, Netherlandish
The National Gallery, London, England*

ST. PETER *the* APOSTLE

Jesus told Peter that he would be given the keys to the kingdom of heaven. Painters often show Peter with a set of keys.

FEAST DAY
June 29

PATRON SAINT
*Fishermen
Rome, Italy*

Peter was a fisherman who loved and followed Jesus. Peter is probably the best known of all the disciples and became not only their leader but the leader of the Christian church.

Peter, who was first known as Simon, lived near the Sea of Galilee. One day, as he and his brother Andrew were fishing, Jesus passed by and asked them to follow him. Jesus gave Simon the name of Peter, which means "rock," saying that he was the rock on which God's church would be built.

Peter was always at Jesus' side, and he saw him perform many miracles. When Peter and the disciples were in a boat on the stormy waters of the Sea of Galilee, they saw Jesus walking across the water. Peter, an eager, warmhearted man, jumped out of the boat to meet his master and found that he, too, could walk on the water! But suddenly he panicked and began to sink before Jesus came to his aid.

Jesus loved Peter and saw a great strength in him, but sometimes the disciple let him down. One night Peter denied ever knowing Jesus and deserted him after Jesus' arrest. But after the resurrection Jesus forgave Peter and asked him to lead his church.

Peter traveled far and wide, telling all types of people about Jesus and, with God's help, performed miracles, too. Years later he arrived in Rome, Italy. At this time Christians were persecuted, and in about A.D. 64 Peter was arrested and crucified. His tomb is said to lie in St. Peter's Basilica in the Vatican in Rome.

SAINT PETER PREACHING
*Pedro Serra (1300s)
Fine Art Museum, Bilbao, Spain*

ST. PAUL *the* APOSTLE

After years spent persecuting Christians, Paul had a blinding vision and was converted to Christianity. He was one of the most important missionaries and founders of the Christian church.

FEAST DAY
June 29

PATRON SAINT
Missionaries
Tent makers

Paul, who was first called Saul, was a Roman citizen who had been taught by the Greeks. He was also a Jew who followed his religion strictly. He had never met Jesus and did not believe he was the Messiah. Saul hated the Christians, and he had many of them arrested. He wanted to stamp out this new religion.

One day, when he was riding to the city of Damascus in modern-day Syria, Saul was blinded by a bright light. He heard the voice of Jesus ask, "Saul, why are you persecuting me?" Saul was led into Damascus where, three days later, Jesus restored his sight. Saul realized that Jesus truly was the Messiah and was baptized. From that day on he was known as Paul.

St. Paul is often shown holding a book and a sword.

Paul became a great preacher and writer and an important missionary. He traveled tirelessly for many years, performing miracles and spreading the word of Jesus. He wrote letters to his new Christian groups, offering encouragement and advice.

Paul had many adventures and was often in trouble. He was beaten, imprisoned, stoned, and shipwrecked, but he never lost his faith. Finally, he was arrested and sent to Rome, Italy. There he is believed to have been beheaded with a sword and buried outside the city walls.

SAINT PAUL ON THE ROAD TO DAMASCUS
Lodovico Carracci (1555–1619)
Pinacoteca Nazionale, Bologna, Italy

SAINT PAUL
Tommaso Masaccio (1401–1428)
Museo di San Matteo, Pisa, Italy

St. Andrew

FEAST DAY
November 30

PATRON SAINT
*Fishermen
Fish dealers
Greece
Russia
Scotland*

Andrew was one of Jesus' 12 disciples and also one of his closest friends. Less well-known than his brother, Peter, Andrew followed Jesus all his life, and, like him, he died on a cross.

Andrew was a fisherman and a follower of John the Baptist. When John told people that Jesus was the Messiah, Andrew believed him and followed Jesus. One day Jesus saw Andrew and his brother fishing and asked them to become his disciples, saying, "I will make you fishers of men." Andrew answered Jesus' call and urged his brother, Peter, to join him.

Andrew saw his master perform many miracles. One day Jesus was preaching to a huge crowd of people who were very hungry. Andrew found a boy with five loaves of bread and two fish and took the food to his master. Jesus miraculously used it to feed more than 5,000 people!

Little is known about Andrew's later life. It is thought he became a missionary and was crucified on an X-shaped cross. It is said that he preached for two entire days before he eventually died.

SAINT ANDREW
*Carlo Crivelli (c. 1430/1435–1494)
The National Gallery, London, England*

St. Thomas

The disciple Thomas found it so hard to believe that Jesus had risen from the dead that, almost 2,000 years after his own death, he is still known as "Doubting Thomas."

FEAST DAY
July 3

PATRON SAINT
*Architects
The blind
India
Pakistan*

Thomas was one of Jesus' disciples. After Jesus rose from the dead he appeared to his disciples—but Thomas was not there. Later, when Thomas heard the amazing news, he simply could not believe it. He declared, "Unless I see in his hands the print of the nails and place my finger in their mark and place my hand in his side, I will not believe."

Poor Thomas! He must have felt very ashamed when he saw Jesus one week later, and his master invited him to touch his wounds. Jesus gently forgave Thomas, but he said, "Blessed are they that have not seen and yet have believed."

Not much more is known about Thomas. He is said to have been a missionary in India and is believed to have been killed with a spear.

THE INCREDULITY OF SAINT THOMAS
Giovanni Battista Cima da Conegliano (c. 1459–1517)
The National Gallery, London, England

19

ST. MATTHEW

FEAST DAY

September 21

PATRON SAINT

Accountants
Bookkeepers
Tax collectors

Once hated as a tax collector, Matthew became one of Jesus' disciples. He is best known as the writer of the first book of the New Testament—the Gospel according to St. Matthew.

Matthew, who lived in Galilee, was a tax collector. Tax collectors were hated and shunned by people and were banned from some temple services. The fact that the taxes went to the Romans made matters even worse. In spite of this, Jesus called on Matthew to become one of his most trusted friends.

Matthew gave up a well-paid job to spend all of his time

with Jesus. Years later, long after Jesus had died, Matthew wrote down everything he could remember about Jesus' life. His writings became the first of the four gospels.

No one knows exactly how Matthew's life ended. Legend tells us he preached in Ethiopia, Africa, where he died for his faith.

SAINT MATTHEW THE EVANGELIST
from a 12th-century Byzantine evangelistary
Biblioteca Nazionale, Marciana, Venice, Italy

St. Mark

Mark was a companion of the disciples Peter and Paul, and he worked alongside the early missionaries. He was a fascinating man and the author of the second gospel.

Mark is usually shown holding his gospel. His other special symbol is a winged lion.

FEAST DAY
April 25

PATRON SAINT
Venice, Italy

Mark lived in the city of Jerusalem. He was the son of a wealthy and important woman, who was one of the first Christians. Her house was a meeting place for the disciples, and Mark often met them. He soon became interested in what they had to say and was baptized a Christian.

Mark decided to become a missionary, traveling first with the disciple Paul and later with his cousin, Barnabas. When Mark eventually arrived in Rome, Italy, he became a close companion of Peter. Years later, when Mark wrote his gospel, he put in the stories that Peter had told him about the life and teachings of Jesus.

Mark's later life is shrouded in legend. It is said that he sailed to Egypt but was captured and killed. Around 700 years later, in A.D. 829, his remains were taken to Venice, Italy, where, it is said, they still lie today inside the famous St. Mark's Basilica.

MARK THE EVANGELIST
Michele di Matteo da Bologna (traceable 1410–1447)
Galleria dell'Accademia, Venice, Italy

ST. LUKE

Luke's symbol is an ox—the animal of sacrifice— because Luke's gospel begins with Zechariah's sacrifice in the temple.

LUKE THE
EVANGELIST
*Agnolo Bronzino
(1503–1572)
Cappella Capponi,
Santa Felicità,
Florence, Italy*

FEAST DAY
October 18

PATRON SAINT
*Artists
Craftspeople
Doctors
Surgeons*

A doctor, a historian, and a fine writer, Luke had many talents. He was the author of the simple but moving account of Jesus' birth that millions of us know today.

Luke was a Greek doctor who lived in the ancient city of Antioch. He was baptized by some of the first missionaries several years after Jesus' death and resurrection.

Luke was a great friend of Paul and traveled with him on two of his missionary journeys. When Paul was arrested and sent to Rome, Italy, Luke decided to go with him. During the voyage their ship broke up in stormy seas. But with God's help, Paul, Luke, and every crew member managed to swim to shore.

Luke was a great writer with a gentle heart. The stories he told showed how Jesus cared for everyone—for women and men, non-Jews and Jews, and for people who were poor and sick.

Luke lived to be very old. As well as writing the Third Gospel, he wrote a history of the early Christian church, which he called the Acts of the Apostles. He is believed to have died peacefully in Boeotia in ancient Greece.

St. John

Once a follower of John the Baptist, John left behind a content fisherman's life to become a disciple of Jesus. In later years he wrote down everything he had seen in the Gospel according to St. John.

John and his older brother, James, were successful fishermen in Galilee. But when Jesus called them to become his disciples, they turned their backs on their work.

John spent a lot of time with Jesus and became one of his most devoted friends—so much so that, moments before he died, Jesus asked John to take care of his mother, Mary.

In later years John suffered hardship and imprisonment as he helped to build the Christian church. After traveling in Turkey and Greece he went to Rome, Italy, where the emperor had him thrown into boiling oil. Miraculously, John survived. In his last years he returned to Turkey, where he worked on his gospel. John was over 90 years old when he died.

FEAST DAY
October 27

PATRON SAINT
Bookbinders
Printers
Theologians
Writers

detail from MADONNA DELL "UMILTA"
Giovanni da Bologna (1300s)
Galleria dell'Accademia, Venice, Italy

23

ST. STEPHEN

Stephen was the first Christian martyr—the first person ever to die for the Christian faith. He lived at a time when it was dangerous to be a Christian, and he was sentenced to a brutal death.

Stephen is often shown with stones, the symbols of his martyrdom.

Stephen was a helper in the early Christian church. He was one of seven people chosen by the apostles to help them spread the message of Jesus and take care of the poor. Stephen was a very special person. As well as being a devoted Christian, he was a wise and educated man. He gave inspiring talks and attracted many followers.

Stephen encouraged many people to become Christians. He explained that Jesus had died to save people from their sins and had risen again to show his power over death. Stephen said that people who believed in Jesus would have eternal life.

Sadly, Stephen made powerful enemies among the Jewish elders. They did not believe that Jesus was the Messiah, and they hated the new Christian church. Again and again they argued with Stephen, but he patiently stood his ground. In the end they made up charges against Stephen and took him to the Jewish court.

In the courtroom Stephen criticized his accusers for not believing in Jesus. Looking up, he told them he could see a vision of Jesus with God in heaven. This angered the court so much that it ordered Stephen to be stoned to death. In this cruel and violent way he became the first Christian martyr.

DATES
Died around A.D. 34–35

FEAST DAY
December 26

PATRON SAINT
*Builders
Deacons*

SAINT STEPHEN
*Il Francia (Francesco di Marco Raibolini) (1450–1517)
Galleria Borghese, Rome, Italy*

St. Sebastian

Sebastian was a Roman soldier with a deadly secret—he was a Christian. He lived at a time when the emperor, Diocletian, was persecuting Christians. Sebastian risked his life inside the enemy camp to help his fellow believers.

Sebastian was a double agent. While he appeared to be one of the emperor's loyal guards, secretly he was comforting Christian prisoners and converting prison guards.

The emperor, who admired Sebastian, asked him to be one of his personal bodyguards. But when he discovered Sebastian's true faith, Diocletian was furious and ordered him to be shot with arrows. The execution was carried out and Sebastian was left for dead, but a woman named Irene found him still alive and nursed him back to health.

With great courage Sebastian returned to the emperor

and protested against his cruelty. Diocletian ordered him to be clubbed to death. This time Sebastian died of his wounds. A church now stands on the spot outside Rome, Italy, where he is believed to be buried.

SAINT SEBASTIAN
Gerrit van
Honthorst
(1592–1056)
The National
Gallery, London,
England

SAINT SEBASTIAN
Raphael, originally Raffaello Sanzio (1483–1520)
Accademia Carrara, Bergamo, Italy

St. Catherine *of* Alexandria

FEAST DAY

November 25

PATRON SAINT

*Librarians
Preachers
Scholars
Young girls
Millers,
spinners,
potters, and
anyone else
who works
with wheels*

The story of Catherine is shrouded in legend. The story goes that this wealthy, educated, and fearless young woman was angered by Roman persecution of the Christians and actually challenged Emperor Maxentius himself!

Catherine lived in Alexandria, a city in Egypt under Roman rule. When Emperor Maxentius heard that she was speaking out about his treatment of the Christians, he sent 50 scholars to convert her back to pagan gods. But Catherine argued with the scholars and converted them to Christianity! A furious Maxentius tried to win Catherine over by asking her to marry him. She refused, saying that she was a "bride of Christ." Later she was imprisoned and ordered to be tortured on a wheel of spikes. But the wheel broke, and Maxentius had her beheaded instead. Catherine's faith was stronger than scholars, the promise of riches, or the fear of death. Her body was taken to Mount Sinai in Egypt, where a shrine to her still stands today.

detail from SAINT CATHERINE OF ALEXANDRIA AND SAINT DOMINIC
Carlo Crivelli (c. 1430/1435–1494)
The National Gallery, London, England

St. Agnes

The legend of St. Agnes tells of a young girl who was so devoted to Christ that she decided to never get married. Christians like Agnes faced persecution from the Romans, and her decision cost Agnes her life.

Agnes is believed to have lived in Rome, Italy, around A.D. 340–350. As the beautiful, young daughter of a wealthy family many men wanted to marry her. However, Agnes refused them all, saying, "Christ is my bridegroom. He was the first to choose me. I shall be his alone." One man who had hoped to marry Agnes was so angry at this refusal that he told the Romans about her. Soon after Agnes was arrested and ordered to give up her Christian beliefs. She bravely and calmly stood by her faith and chose to be executed instead. Roman writers of the time praised Agnes for the incredible courage she showed.

detail from THE CRUCIFIXION WITH SAINTS
Master of Liesbon (mid- to late 1400s)
The National Gallery, London, England

29

FEAST DAY
January 21

PATRON SAINT
Engaged couples
Gardeners
Young girls

In paintings St. Agnes is often shown with a lamb—a symbol of purity and innocence. The name Agnes comes from the Latin word for a lamb, agnus.

St. Christopher

FEAST DAY
July 25

PATRON SAINT
Drivers
Sailors
Travelers

The legend of St. Christopher is very well-known. It explains how a very strong man struggled to carry a child across a river. This, of course, was no ordinary child—it was Jesus Christ.

Christopher was a huge man—in fact, he was more like a giant. He lived by a river and worked as a ferryman, carrying people across the water. Christopher had learned about Jesus Christ and hoped to meet him. One night a small child asked Christopher to carry him over the water. As the giant waded into the river the water became deeper, and the child grew so heavy that Christopher feared they would drown. When they reached the other side, the child told him he was Jesus Christ, who "carried the weight of the whole world on his shoulders."

Legend says that Christopher later traveled to Turkey to tell people about Jesus. There he was imprisoned and treated very harshly. He was beaten, shot with arrows, and was finally beheaded.

ST. CHRISTOPHER
Dieric Bouts the Elder (c. 1410/1420–1475)
Alte Pinakothek, Munich, Germany

St. Cecilia

Cecilia was said to hear heavenly music whenever she prayed to God. For her, music brought strength and comfort. It helped her live through dangerous times and face a cruel death.

DATES
A.D. 100s and 200s

FEAST DAY
November 22

PATRON SAINT
Composers
Music
Musicians
Organ builders
Singers

The story of Cecilia, who was born in Rome, Italy, is little more than legend. At an early age she devoted herself to God. When she was promised in marriage to a man named Valerian, she was very unhappy. She prayed to God and was comforted by the sound of heavenly music.

Valerian was a good man. He understood why Cecilia did not want a husband, and he not only respected her wishes but became a Christian too. At this time Christians were executed daily by the Roman authorities. When Valerian and his brother Tiburtius were discovered burying these Christian martyrs, they were also executed.

Cecilia never tried to hide her faith. She preached openly and converted people to Christianity. In time she was arrested and was later beheaded. As the sword struck Cecilia sang to God and comforted herself with music.

SAINT CECILIA WITH AN ANGEL
Orazio Gentileschi (1563–1640)
Galleria Nazionale dell'Umbria, Perugia, Italy

31

St. Joan of Arc

At a time when France was at war with England a young French girl answered God's call and led her country to victory. She followed her conscience in the face of death and, years later, was made a saint.

Joan of Arc, the youngest daughter of a poor farmer, grew up in a small French village and never learned to read or write. In 1425, at the age of 13, she began to hear voices who she said were those of saints. They commanded her to drive out the English army from France—surely an impossible task for a young girl!

But Joan was determined to follow God's will. Although she suffered many setbacks, she impressed people with her devotion and courage. When she met Charles, the crown prince of France, he gave her a small army. In April 1429, at the age of 17, she led her troops to a famous victory against the English and freed the city of Orléans.

Joan, inspired by her voices, won victory in five more battles. By chance she was captured and sold to the English. They wanted to get rid of her and charged her with witchcraft. At her trial Joan spoke bravely about her voices and her calling from God, but the English sent her to a terrible death. On May 30, 1431 Joan was burned at the stake in the marketplace in Rouen, France, and her ashes were thrown into the Seine River. Joan was made a saint 500 years later.

JOAN OF ARC AT THE CORONATION OF KING CHARLES VII
Jean-Auguste Dominique Ingres (1780–1867)
Musée du Louvre, Paris, France

JOAN OF ARC—
detail from the
c. 1505 manuscript
"La Vie des
Femmes Celebres"
(Life of Famous
Women)
Antoine du Four
Musze Thomas
Dobrze, Nantes,
France

FEAST DAY
May 30

PATRON SAINT
France
Soldiers

St. Augustine

DATES
A.D. 354–430

S t. Augustine is one of the most important figures of the Christian church. A brilliant man, he is famous not for the things he did but for the things he thought and wrote.

SAINT AUGUSTINE
Nicoletto Semitecolo
(1300s)
Santa Maria dei
Servi, Venice, Italy

Augustine was born in North Africa to a Christian mother and a pagan father. He was brought up as a Christian, but as he grew older he lost interest in leading a good life and put aside his Christian faith. Augustine studied public speaking. When he was around 30, he went to Rome, Italy, and taught there as a professor. Yet he felt something important was missing from his life. He met with priests and bishops and became interested in Christianity again. He was converted very suddenly in his garden one evening after reading some words by St. Paul.

FEAST DAY
August 28

PATRON SAINT
Theologians

Augustine returned to North Africa and set up a monastery there. For the rest of his life, as a monk, a priest, and the Bishop of Hippo, he preached to people and cared for the poor—but most of all he wrote. He wrote about his sinful past, his search for God, and about the history and teachings of Christianity. These writings have inspired and helped Christians for many hundreds of years.

detail from SAINT AUGUSTINE AND THE CHILD ON THE SEASHORE
Pinturicchio (1454–1513)
Galleria Nazionale dell'Umbria, Perugia, Italy

St. Patrick

St. Patrick was a humble man who had great energy and enthusiasm. He spent 25 years converting the Irish people to Christianity at a time when Ireland seemed pagan and wild. He is now the most popular Irish saint.

Patrick, first known as Patricius, was born in Roman Great Britain. His father was a Roman citizen, and his grandfather was a Christian priest. Patrick was only a teenager when his life took a dramatic turn. He was captured by pirates, taken to Ireland, and sold as a slave. For six years he worked for an Irish chief, taking care of sheep and pigs. Lonely, unhappy, and longing to escape, he prayed to God every day and night.

Eventually Patrick escaped from slavery and boarded a boat to France. There, he had many more adventures before finally returning home. Patrick then decided to train to become a priest. Although he was not well educated, he was deeply caring and sincere. His early years—as an exile, a slave, and a runaway—had taught him to trust God completely.

In A.D. 435 Patrick was made Bishop of Ireland. To outsiders Ireland seemed like the edge of the world. It did not belong to the Roman Empire, and Christianity was hardly known. Patrick was a very successful missionary. He converted Irish chiefs, set up monasteries, and organized the growing church. He died around 461 and has since become the best loved of the Irish saints.

Dates
*c. A.D.
385–461*

Feast Day
March 17

Patron Saint
Ireland

The miracle of St. Patrick of Ireland
*Giovanni Battista Tiepolo (1696–1770)
Museo Civico, Padua, Italy*

St. Thomas Aquinas

The sun is one of St. Thomas' symbols, as well as a chalice and an ox.

DATES
1225–1274

FEAST DAY
January 28

PATRON SAINT
Academics
Philosophers
Schools and
colleges
Theologians

Thomas Aquinas was a large, silent man, nicknamed the "dumb ox" by his fellow students. Yet he proved to be one of the most important thinkers, writers, and teachers the Christian church has ever known.

Thomas Aquinas was born into a wealthy Italian family and had a fantastic education. Yet, to the horror of his parents, he decided to become a monk.

As a monk Thomas continued to study, and his teachers were the best of the age. Soon he was writing and lecturing at universities in Italy and France.

Thomas' works are masterpieces of clear thinking and powerful arguments—about the Bible and Christian teachings and ideas. He wrote so much and worked so hard that he is said to have dictated his ideas to four different secretaries at one time!

Overwork led to Thomas' death at the early age of 49. Yet, 1,500 years later, his writings are still studied by theology students and would-be priests today.

St. Thomas Aquinas
Gentile da Fabriano (c. 1370–1427)
Pinacoteca di Brera, Milan, Italy

St. Teresa of Avila

Teresa was a Spanish nun who devoted her life to poverty and prayer. She set up convents all over Spain, and the books and letters she wrote for her nuns are still widely read today.

Teresa had many visions. In one she is believed to have seen a dove. This has become one of her symbols.

DATES
1515–1582

FEAST DAY
October 15

PATRON SAINT
Lace makers

The daughter of noble parents, Teresa was born in Avila, Spain. When she was a teenager, her mother died, and she decided to become a nun. The convent she joined was very easygoing, with frequent visitors from town. Teresa longed to live a simpler, more disciplined life. She spent many hours in deep prayer and began to have holy visions.

Teresa suffered years of poor health. When she recovered, she started a convent away from the distractions of the world. Here, Teresa and her nuns spent many hours alone with God in prayer. The rest of the time was spent doing simple chores such as sweeping and sewing. Though life was strict, Teresa was a warm, cheerful woman and was greatly loved by her nuns. In time she started 16 more convents. She wrote letters of encouragement to them all, and her books about a life of prayer are still inspiring to read.

TERESA OF AVILA'S VISION OF A DOVE
Peter Paul Rubens (1577–1640)
Fitzwilliam Museum, University of Cambridge, England

ST. FRANCIS *of* ASSISI

DATES
1181–1226

FEAST DAY
October 4

PATRON SAINT
*Animals
Ecologists
Italy*

St. Francis gave up a life of wealth and comfort to help and care for the poor. He is a popular saint, particularly with children, and is fondly remembered for his love of animals and all of God's creations.

Francis lived in Assisi, Italy, and was the son of a wealthy merchant. He was expected to go into his family's business, but he was more interested in helping the poor and sick. One day he sold some of his father's goods and gave money to a ruined church. His father was so angry that Francis stripped off his rich clothes and turned his back on his family forever.

His new life was one of poverty and prayer. He traveled from place to place, preaching and caring for the sick and living on what people gave him. He devotedly nursed a man with leprosy—an illness that was greatly feared at the time—and publicly kissed the man's hand. Francis' strength and courage inspired people to follow him, and in time he formed a group of monks known as the Franciscans.

Toward the end of his life Francis had a vision of Christ on the cross. When it was over, Francis found that his hands and feet were bleeding, just like the crucified Christ's. These wounds, known as stigmata, lasted until Francis' death.

SAINT FRANCIS
*Giovanni da Milano (1320–1369)
Musée du Louvre, Paris, France*

SAINT FRANCIS OF ASSISI GIVES CLOAK TO POOR HORSEMAN
*Giotto di Bondone (1200–1337)
Upper Church of S. Francesco, Assisi, Italy*

St. Elizabeth *of* Hungary

Elizabeth was a royal princess, and her crown has become her symbol.

Dates
1207–1231

Feast day
November 17

Patron saint
Bakers
Beggars
Charities
Lace makers

For most of her short life Elizabeth knew only wealth and happiness. When that happiness came to a sudden end, she turned her back on her comfortable life and devoted herself to the poor.

Elizabeth was the daughter of the king of Hungary. When she was only four years old, she was engaged to a prince named Louis and was sent to live in Germany. Elizabeth grew up to love Louis. Years later they married and had three children.

Elizabeth was a beautiful, compassionate woman and was very generous to the poor. Her life took a tragic turn when Louis suddenly died of the plague. Elizabeth was heartbroken. She was thrown out of her home by Louis' brother and decided to join a Franciscan order of nuns.

She then lived a life of poverty, helping the poor and sick. She had a harsh spiritual teacher, who slapped her and beat her with sticks to keep her "holy," but it only made her weak and ill. She died when she was only 24.

St. Elizabeth of Hungary spinning wool for the poor
Marianne Stokes (1855–1927)
Private Collection

St. Rose *of* Lima

St. Rose was the first saint of the Americas. This beautiful young woman was not interested in marriage. Instead, she lived a life of holiness and hardship and dedicated herself to God.

Rose was the daughter of a Spanish family who lived in Lima, Peru. Unlike most women, she hated her beauty—she rubbed her face with pepper and cut off all her hair. Even though Rose had many admirers, she decided to become a nun. She lived in a hut in her garden at home and spent many hours praying.

Rose believed that the more she suffered, the closer she could be to God. She wore a crown of roses and dug their thorns into her head. She wore a dress made of the roughest cloth. She fasted several times each week and would not drink to quench her thirst. Sadly, she became weak and, after a long illness, died when she was only 31.

Rose is a popular saint. Huge crowds lined the streets at her funeral, and her home has become a shrine.

The rose is linked with St. Rose's name and has become her symbol.

DATES
1586–1617

FEAST DAY
August 23

PATRON SAINT
*Florists
Gardeners
Peru
South America*

detail from MARY WITH THE THREE HOLY DOMINICAN NUNS CATHERINE OF SIENA, ROSE OF LIMA, AND AGNES OF MONTEPULCINO
*Giovanni Battista Tiepolo (1696–1770)
S. Maria del Rosario, Venice, Italy*

St. Nicholas

DATES
A.D. 300s

FEAST DAY
December 6

PATRON SAINT
*Children
Merchants
Russia
Sailors
Unmarried
women*

Legend tells us that St. Nicholas was a sweet, kind, generous man who liked to help people in need. He is known around the world as "Santa Claus" and is one of the most popular saints of all.

We know very little about St. Nicholas. He was a bishop who lived in Myra, Turkey, at some time during the A.D. 300s. There are many different stories about him. In one he is said to have helped three young sisters who were too poor to marry. Nicholas crept by their house one night and threw three bags of gold through a window. This was a secret, generous act that asked for nothing in return. Stories about St. Nicholas have spread from one country to another. It was the Dutch who first shortened his name to "Claus" and called him Santa Claus. Today he has become the secret visitor who leaves presents for good children. In some countries children receive presents on his feast day; in others, on Christmas Eve.

detail from THE PERUGIA ALTARPIECE
*Fra Angelico (c. 1387–1455)
Galleria Nazionale dell'Umbria, Perugia, Italy*

ST. BERNADETTE

Bernadette was a poor girl from Lourdes, France, who had visions of the Virgin Mary. These visions have made her hometown an important place of Christian pilgrimage.

Bernadette was only 14 years old when she had a vision of the Virgin Mary. Over the next six months she had many more. In the visions Mary spoke to Bernadette, led her to a spring of healing water, and asked her to build a church.

Priests were suspicious about Bernadette's visions and questioned her for many years. She stood by her story and was finally believed. A church was built on the site of her visions, and it was said that the nearby spring was a place of healing.

Bernadette was quiet and humble and did not enjoy the attention. She entered a convent, where she worked and prayed. She had always suffered from asthma and poor health and was only 35 when she died.

DATES
1844–1879

FEAST DAY
April 16

PATRON SAINT
Shepherdesses

BERNADETTE SOUBIROUS
French School (1900s)
Biblioteque des Arts Decoratifs, Paris, France

45

AMERICAN SAINTS

Although the United States is a young country, its history is filled with stories of Americans who have dedicated their lives to God.

St. Frances Xavier Cabrini (1850–1917)
Known as the "patroness of immigrants," Francesca Maria Cabrini was born on a farm in Italy, the youngest of 13 children. She dreamed of becoming a missionary but became a teacher instead. After her parents died a local priest asked Frances to run a girls' school and orphanage that was in great need of attention. Six years later she founded a mission to take care of poor children in schools and hospitals around Italy. As news of Frances' good works spread the pope asked her to go to New York City to care for the Italian immigrants there, who were suffering under miserable living and working conditions. This was the first of many long sea journeys for Frances, resulting in the establishment of more than 1,000 missions in eight countries, involved in hospitals, orphanages, and schools. She was tireless in her love for children but died alone and suddenly at the age of 67, physically worn out. Frances was the first U.S. citizen to be made a saint when she was canonized in 1946.

St. Katharine Drexel (1858–1955)

St. Katharine was the daughter of a wealthy Philadelphia family and inherited a huge fortune. Her parents taught her to be thankful for her wealth and to use it to help the most oppressed members of society. Katharine became particularly concerned about the treatment of blacks and Native Americans. Despite much

opposition from segregationists, she used her inheritance
to found the Sisters of the Blessed Sacrament and to establish
more than 60 missions to provide education for Native and
African-Americans. She also set up the only Catholic university
for blacks in the U.S.—Xavier University in New Orleans.
She was canonized in 2000.

St. Elizabeth Ann Bayley Seton (1774–1821)

Elizabeth was born in New York City into a prominent family.
Despite her "high society" life, Elizabeth was
often sad and lonely and found comfort in
the Bible. She married a rich merchant
and had five children, but within ten
years her husband's health and fortune
declined. They moved to Italy hoping
to find a cure, but in 1803 he died
there. Elizabeth was drawn to Roman
Catholicism, and when she returned
to the U.S., she was admitted to the
Catholic church, despite anger from
family and friends. She then started
a Catholic girls' school in Baltimore.
Elizabeth also founded orphanages,
hospitals, and schools and still found
time to spend with the poor and sick
and to write hymns and compose
music. She was the first native-born
American to be canonized in 1975.

ST. ELIZABETH
ANN BAYLEY
SETON'S
FEAST DAY
January 4

WHAT ARE ANGELS?

Angels are God's messengers. In the Bible these beautiful beings are sent from heaven to people on earth to deliver help, warnings, or exciting news.

Angels are holy beings that were created by God and have direct contact with the creator. The word "angel" comes from the Greek word *angelos*, which means messenger. Their appearances in the Bible are brief but important; they are a link between heaven and earth.

In the Bible angels appear in different ways. Sometimes they appear in a blaze of glory, dazzling onlookers and filling them with fear. This is how the angels appeared to the shepherds in Bethlehem on the night that Jesus was born: "And, lo, the angel of the Lord came upon them, and the glory of the Lord shone around about them: and they were sore afraid."

detail from POLYPTYCH OF THE DOMINICANS, CUSP: ANNOUNCING ANGEL
Fra Angelico (c. 1387–1455)
Galleria Nazionale dell'Umbria, Perugia, Italy

Angels sometimes appear to people while they are asleep. An angel appeared to Joseph in his dreams to tell him that Mary was expecting the Son of God. At other times angels take a human form. In the Old Testament Abraham meets three strangers, whom he invites into his tent

BIRTH OF CHRIST
*Robert Campin
(Master of Flemalle)
(c.1375/1380–1444)
Muée des Beaux-Arts,
Dijon, France*

for a meal. It is only when they tell him that his wife, Sarah, will have a child that he realizes they are really angels.

As well as delivering important messages, angels also provide practical help. At times they protect those who show obedience to God; in the Old Testament an angel protects Daniel when he is thrown into a lions' den. At other times they protect those who do God's work; in the New Testament an angel frees Peter from prison by breaking his prison chains.

The Bible tells us that angels worship only God. They are happy when people come to know and love God. In fact, when humans die, angels are said to welcome them and carry them into heaven.

GUARDIAN ANGELS

ST. PETER FREED
FROM PRISON
*Sebastiano Ricci
(1658–1734)
Santa Stae,
Venice, Italy*

Some Christians believe that guardian angels exist to help and protect us. They suggest that, at the moment of our birth, each of us is given a guardian angel to accompany us through life. This comforting idea has existed for many thousands of years and is even mentioned in the Bible.

When Peter the apostle is thrown into prison by Herod Antipas, his fellow Christians pray for his safety. These prayers are heard by God, who sends an angel to the prison. The angel removes Peter's chains. At first Peter thinks it is all a dream, but when the angel leads him to freedom, he realizes that the angel was sent by God to deliver him from Herod.

Some Christians believe that guardian angels are always there to help us—they are our partners on the path to heaven. People can call on angels to protect them in their struggle to lead good lives.

CHOIRS OF ANGELS

Countless angels are said to exist in heaven. This fact once fascinated Christians so much that they attempted to sort these heavenly beings into groups. Some groups of angels had specific roles and were said to perform particular tasks.

The highest group are the archangels. Only three—Michael, Gabriel, and Raphael—are named in the Bible, even though Raphael says he is one of seven. The archangels are powerful beings who are very close to God and have the authority to bring about great change.

Two other groups of angels are the cherubim and seraphim. They are said to surround and worship the throne of heaven

and to serve God day and night. The Book of Genesis tells us that when Adam and Eve were banished from the Garden of Eden, God sent the cherubim to guard the Tree of Life.

There is an important difference between the archangels and the cherubim and seraphim. Archangels have contact with people on earth; cherubim and seraphim do not.

ANGELS
*Benozzo Gozzoli
(1420–1497)
Palazzo
Medici-Riccardi,
Cappella dei Magi,
Florence, Italy*

ARCHANGEL MICHAEL

Michael is God's most trusted creature and carries out heaven's commands. A fierce warrior, protector, and comforting guardian, Michael is the greatest angel of all.

Michael is heaven's most powerful archangel. In the Old Testament Daniel calls Michael "one of the chief princes" and believes this angel to be the guardian of the Israelites. The very name, Michael, means "who is like God"—a good name for an angel who acts with great authority, almost as an assistant to God.

Michael is a champion of goodness and justice and fights evil at every chance. When one of God's angels, Lucifer, started a war in heaven (*see* pages 58–59), Michael fought and defeated the rebels and threw them out of heaven. No wonder Michael is known as the "warrior angel" and is often painted wearing a full suit of armor.

There are several legends about Michael. It is said that this angel appeared in Rome, Italy, when there was a horrible plague. This may be why Michael is said to protect the sick and receive their souls into heaven. Michael is also believed to be a guardian of high places. Two monasteries dedicated to Michael—St. Michael's Mount in Great Britain and Mont St. Michel in France—were both built on outcrops of rock.

FEAST DAY
September 29—
known as
"St. Michael and
all the angels"

PATRON
Brussels, Belgium
Police officers
The sick

THE ARCHANGEL MICHAEL
Pietro Perugina (1469–1523)
The National Gallery, London, England

ARCHANGEL GABRIEL

The name Gabriel means "the hero of God."

FEAST DAY

September 29

PATRON

*Broadcasters
Messengers
Postal workers
Telecommunication
workers
Writers*

The archangel Gabriel is the best known of all the angels. Gabriel is the angel who appears to Mary and tells her the exciting news that she is going to have a baby who will be the Son of God.

Gabriel is mentioned several times in the Bible, and he is always the bringer of important news. In the Old Testament this angel appears to Daniel in the form of a man. Gabriel helps Daniel understand a puzzling vision and prophesies the coming of Jesus.

In the New Testament Gabriel appears to Zechariah, saying, "I am Gabriel who stands in the presence of God." The angel tells Zechariah that he will have a son named John who will grow up to be a great prophet—the famous John the Baptist. Zechariah is so frightened that he is speechless with shock! A few months later God sends Gabriel to tell Mary about the birth of Jesus—the Son of God.

Many artists have painted the scene where Gabriel tells Mary about the birth of Jesus. This is known as the Annunciation.

THE ANNUNCIATION
*Zanobi Strozzi (c. 1395–1455)
The National Gallery, London, England*

THE ANNUNCIATION: THE ANGEL GABRIEL
*Ferrari Gaudenzio (c. 1508–1546)
The National Gallery, London, England*

ARCHANGEL RAPHAEL

The name Raphael means "God heals." In a wonderful story this caring archangel shows a young man named Tobias how to cure his father's blindness.

ANGEL
*Raphael, originally
Raffaello Sanzio,
(1483–1520)
Pinacota Civica
T. Martinengo,
Brescia, Italy*

FEAST DAY
September 29

PATRON
*The blind
Doctors
Nurses
Travelers*

There is a story about Raphael and a man named Tobit, who lived long before Jesus was born. Tobit was a good man who helped the poor, but one night he suddenly lost his sight. His blindness was a great burden to him, and he prayed to God to let him die. God heard his prayers and sent Raphael to help.

Meanwhile Tobit was preparing for death. He asked his son, Tobias, to collect some savings from a place called Media. Raphael appeared to Tobias in human form, explained that he was a distant relative, and went with him on the journey.

One day Tobias caught a fish. Raphael told him to remove its insides, which he said could be used as a cure. Weeks later, when the travelers returned home, Raphael told Tobias to rub the fish on his father's eyes. Miraculously, Tobit's blindness was cured!

Then Raphael revealed his true identity: "I am Raphael, one of the seven holy angels who . . . enter in the presence of the glory of the Holy One." The angel told Tobit and Tobias to praise and thank God, before vanishing and returning to heaven.

detail from THE VIRGIN AND CHILD WITH AN ANGEL, THE ARCHANGEL MICHAEL, AND THE ARCHANGEL RAPHAEL WITH TOBIAS
Pietro Perugino (1469–1523)
The National Gallery, London, England

FALLEN ANGELS

SATAN IS
CHAINED FOR A
THOUSAND YEARS
Juan Gerson
(1500s)
Church of the
Franciscan
monastery,
Tecamachalco,
Mexico

The Bible mentions only four angels by name—Michael, Gabriel, Raphael, and Lucifer. In the beginning they were all good, but one of them, Lucifer, was tempted into sin and became God's enemy.

There is a famous story about the angel Lucifer. Lucifer, whose name means "light bearer," was very, very proud. In time this angel wanted to sit on the throne of heaven and enjoy the power that belonged to God alone. Lucifer must have been very persuasive— soon one third of all the angels agreed to join the rebel angel in the fight against God. This is how war broke out in heaven.

Small parts of this story appear in old translations of the Bible in the Book of Revelation; others have been added by writers over the years. The story goes that the archangel Michael fought Lucifer and the rebel army and, acting on God's will, threw them out of heaven. At this point in the story Lucifer was given a new name—Satan. The fallen archangel was chained up in a dark pit for one thousand years.

Satan tried to tempt people away from God in several Bible stories. When Jesus went into the wilderness for 40 days and nights, Satan encouraged him to challenge God and use his power for his own purposes. Later Satan tempted Jesus' disciple, Judas, to betray his master for 30 pieces of silver. Satan is also known by other names such as Beelzebub and the Prince of Darkness.

THE THREE ARCHANGELS
Marco d'Oggiano (c. 1470–1530)
Pinacoteca di Brera, Milan, Italy

CALENDAR OF FEAST DAYS

indicates the saints featured in this book

JANUARY

2   St. Basil the Great
4   *St. Elizabeth Ann
    Bayley Seton
12 St. Benedict
14 St. Sava
17 St. Anthony Abbot
19 St. Henry of
    Uppsalla
20 *St. Sebastian
21 *St. Agnes
24 St. Francis de
    Sales
28 *St. Thomas
    Aquinas
31 St. John Bosco

FEBRUARY

1   St. Brigid
3   St. Anskar
8   St. Jerome
    Emilian
9   St. Apollonia
14 St. Cyril
    St. Methodius
    St. Valentine
19 St. Boniface
23 St. Polycarp

MARCH

2   St. Chad
3   *St. Katharine
    Drexel
17 *St. Patrick
19 *St. Joseph
20 St. Cuthbert
24 St. Iranaeus,
    Bishop of
    Sirmium

APRIL

4   St. Isidore
11 St. Stanislaus
16 *St. Bernadette
17 St. Stephen
    Harding
23 St. Adalbert
    of Prague
25 *St. Mark
29 St. Catherine
    of Siena
30 St. Pius V

MAY

19 St. Dunstan
27 St. Augustine,
    Archbishop of
    Canterbury
30 *St. Joan of Arc

JUNE

2   St. Erasmus
    (Elmo)
5   St. Boniface
9   St. Columba
11 St. Barnabas
13 St. Anthony
    of Padua
24 *St. John the
    Baptist
28 St. Irenaeus,
    Bishop of
    Lyons

29 *St. Paul
    *St. Peter

JULY

3   *St. Thomas
11 St. Benedict
15 St. Bonaventure
20 St. Margaret
    of Antioch
22 *St. Mary
    Magdalene
23 St. Bridget
    of Sweden
25 *St. Christopher
    St. James the
    Great
26 *St. Anne
    St. Joachim
29 St. Olaf
31 St. Ignatius
    of Loyola

AUGUST

8 St. Dominic
10 St. Lawrence
11 St. Clare
14 St. Maximilian
Kolbe
15 *Virgin Mary
16 St. Stephen
of Hungary
20 St. Bernard
21 St. Pius X
23 *St. Rose of Lima
24 St. Bartholomew

26 St. Ninian
28 *St. Augustine,
Bishop of
Hippo

SEPTEMBER

1 St. Giles

3 St. Gregory
the Great
9 St. Peter Claver
13 St. John
Chrysostom
17 St. Hildegard
21 *St. Matthew
28 St. Wenceslaus
29 All angels
30 St. Jerome

OCTOBER

1 St. Térèse
of Lisieux
4 *St. Francis
of Assisi
6 St. Bruno
9 St. Denis
10 St. Francis
Borgia
13 St. Edward the
Confessor
15 *St. Teresa of Avila
16 St. Gall
18 *St. Luke
19 St. Isaac Jogues
25 St. Crispin
27 *St. John
28 St. Jude
St. Simon

NOVEMBER

1 All Saints' Day
7 St. Willibrord
11 St. Martin
of Tours

13 *St. Frances
Xavier Cabrini
15 St. Albert the
Great
16 St. Margaret
of Scotland
17 *St. Elizabeth
of Hungary
22 *St. Cecilia
23 St. Clement I
25 *St. Catherine
of Alexandria
30 *St. Andrew

DECEMBER

1 St. Edmund
Campion
4 St. Barbara
6 *St. Nicholas
7 St. Ambrose
10 St. Gregory III
13 St. Lucy
19 St. Anastasius I
26 *St. Stephen

27 *St. John the
Apostle
29 St. Thomas à
Becket

GLOSSARY

anoint   to pour oil over someone or something to make it holy

apostle   one who is sent with the authority of Jesus such as the 12 disciples and St. Paul

ascension   Jesus' return to heaven after he had been resurrected

baptize   to use water as a sign of faith, repentance, and washed-away sin, admitting the believer to the Christian church

crucifixion   a form of execution in which a person is nailed to a wooden cross

disciple   anyone who follows and learns from another such as one of the 12 close followers of Jesus

eternal   something that is everlasting, without a beginning or an end

exile   the banishment of someone from their own country

Gospel   one of the first four books of the New Testament that narrate Jesus' life

heaven   the place where God and his angels live and where Christian believers will join God after death

martyr   someone who is ready to suffer and die for his or her faith

miracles   dramatic and surprising events that cannot be explained

missionaries   people who are sent to teach others about their religion

pagan   a person with no religious beliefs or who worships many different gods

persecution   the unfair and cruel treatment of people because of their religion

pilgrimage   a journey to a shrine or other holy place

plague   an infectious disease that spreads quickly and kills many people

prophet   someone who receives messages from God and tells other people about them

resurrection   Jesus' return from death to a new life that would last forever

shrine   a place that is especially holy—for example, the tomb of a saint

theology   the study of religious ideas

visions   revelations from God that show events that have not yet happened

Notable people

Abraham The man chosen by God to be the father of the Israelites. The Israelites were a great nation and were God's chosen people, from whom the Jews were descended.

Barnabas A friend and fellow missionary of St. Paul and St. Mark.

Daniel An exiled Jew who worked in the royal court of Babylon. He was thrown into a lions' den because of his religion, but an angel was sent to protect him.

Diocletian Roman emperor (A.D. 284–305) who ordered the persecution of the Christians.

Elizabeth The wife of Zechariah and mother of John the Baptist.

Herod (the Great) The king of Judea when Jesus was born who ordered all baby boys to be killed.

Herod Antipas One of the sons of Herod the Great. He persecuted many Christians and ordered the beheading of John the Baptist.

Herodias The wife of Herod Antipas, she wanted the death of John the Baptist.

Joachim The husband of Anne, who was Mary's mother.

Judas One of Jesus' 12 disciples. Judas betrayed Jesus to the Romans, leading to Jesus' arrest and death.

Maxentius Roman emperor (A.D. 306–312) who ordered the persecution of the Christians.

Salome The daughter of Herodias. Her dance for Herod Antipas led to the death of John the Baptist.

Sarah The wife of Abraham.

Tobias The son of Tobit, who was accompanied on a journey by the archangel Raphael and who helped cure his father's blindness.

Tobit The father of Tobias, who became blind and was cured by the archangel Raphael.

Zechariah The father of John the Baptist.

INDEX